JUN − 8 2016

Understanding Coding with

LEGO WeDo™

Kids
Can
Code

Patricia Harris

PowerKiDS
press

New York

Published in 2016 by The Rosen Publishing Group, Inc.
29 East 21st Street, New York, NY 10010

First Edition

Editor: Greg Roza
Book Design: Michael J. Flynn

Photo Credits: Cover (boy with laptop) Monkey Business Images/Shutterstock.com; cover (LEGO WeDo alligator) Platz Niederösterreich/www.flickr.com/photos/award2008/6781226205/CC BY 2.0; p. 5 Baloncici/Shutterstock.com; pp. 7, 8, 12–15, 17, 21, 22 (LEGO screenshots and graphics) the LEGO Group; p. 9 www.flickr.com/photos/polytechnicum/17209484215/CC BY-NC 2.0; p. 11 Kevin Jarrett/ www.flickr.com/photos/kjarrett/11029475633/CC BY 2.0; pp. 15, 18, 19 by Michael Flynn; p. 17 (LEGO WeDo alligator) jeanbaptisteparis/www.flickr.com/photos/jeanbaptisteparis/4934422475/CC BY-SA 2.0; p. 20 Brad Flickinger/www.flickr.com/photos/56155476@N08/5675862280/CC BY 2.0.

The LEGO name and products, including MINDSTORMS and WeDo, are trademarks of the LEGO Group, and their use in this book does not imply a recommendation or endorsement of this title by the LEGO Group.

Cataloging-in-Publication Data

Harris, Patricia.
Understanding coding with LEGO WeDo™ / by Patricia Harris.
p. cm. — (Kids can code)
Includes index.
ISBN 978-1-5081-4466-3 (pbk.)
ISBN 978-1-5081-4467-0 (6-pack)
ISBN 978-1-5081-4468-7 (library binding)
1. Computer programming — Juvenile literature. 2. Simple machines — Juvenile literature. 3. Robotics — Juvenile literature. I. Harris, Patricia, 1949-. II. Title.
QA76.73.P98 H37 2016
005.1—d23

Manufactured in the United States of America

CPSIA Compliance Information: Batch #BW16PK: For Further Information contact Rosen Publishing, New York, New York at 1-800-237-9932

Contents

Build and Code

Many people—kids and adults alike—love building with LEGO creations. LEGO blocks have been around since the 1950s. Many special blocks and other parts have been added to the LEGO line over the years. LEGO kits have offered many opportunities for people to learn about building, robotics, and now coding!

WeDo is about using gears and motors. Robots use motors and gears to move themselves around. But the gears and motors only work because a program is written to control them. WeDo is especially fun because it not only allows young coders to learn about coding, but also the **practical** application of code used to control something other than a computer—in this case, a LEGO robot the coder builds himself or herself!

Breaking the Code

WeDo is a LEGO kit that allows you to create the code needed to **automate** robots and **vehicles** you build with LEGO pieces. The easy-to-understand WeDo **environment** is a fun way to learn basic coding concepts. The colorful LEGO blocks, wheels, motors, and sensors help you understand simple robotic principles. Combining the two elements teaches important concepts about robotics and coding in real life.

This commercial robot can use its arms to move items in a warehouse because a computer programmer wrote code to control it. This is what WeDo does, but on a much smaller scale.

LEGO Mechanic

Before you can code, you need to build the robot. The WeDo kit includes motors, sensors, gears, and other building pieces that can be used to make a programmable vehicle or robot. The sensors and motors connect to the connection **module**, and the connection module plugs in to a **USB port** on your computer. This sends power to the robot's sensors and motor, allowing them to function.

The WeDo kit also includes colorful LEGO blocks and even a LEGO minifigure! The kit comes with the parts that will allow your creation to move, change speed, turn, and stop. These parts include gears, wheels, axles, bands, and more. A gearbox is a special set of gears that can move in different ways. Once you add a power source, your creation is ready to roll!

Breaking the Code

A WeDo motion sensor is much like a motion detector on an outdoor light. When something moves in front of the light's detector, the light turns on. When something moves in front of the WeDo motion sensor, the next part of your program starts. The tilt sensor starts the next part of the program when the item it's connected to is tilted in a direction you choose.

The connection module has two special places for the motor and sensors to plug in to. The motor module also has a place to plug in a sensor on top of it so you can have the motor and both sensors connected at the same time.

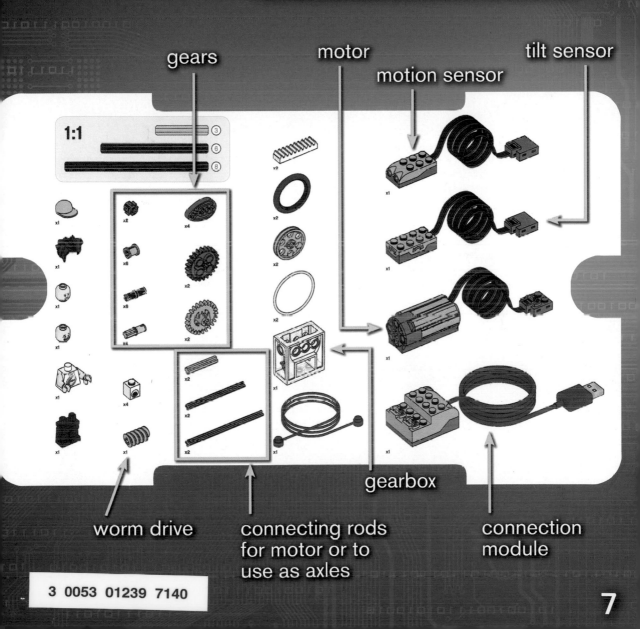

gears

motor

motion sensor

tilt sensor

1:1

gearbox

worm drive

connecting rods for motor or to use as axles

connection module

LEGO Coder

A WeDo kit comes with a CD containing the WeDo **software**. The WeDo **programming language** is very much like the blocks it was designed to control. It features colorful "blocks" that coders can drag and drop into a work area. These blocks fit together to create actions for your LEGO creation to act out. You can make a truck roll forward and turn right. You can make an alligator open its mouth and roar!

start arrow   time block

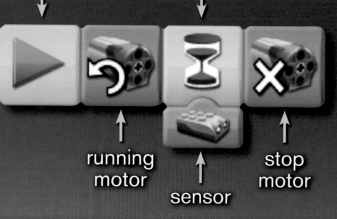

running motor   stop motor

sensor

Here's a simple example of WeDo code. Notice how the separate blocks of code fit together like LEGO blocks. This code tells a motor to keep working until the motion sensor detects motion. Can you tell what each block in the code does from its picture?

Writing code in LEGO WeDo is simple. Just drag instruction blocks into a line to make your items do what you want them to do. LEGO includes several projects in the kit that you can explore when you open the programming language from the WeDo CD.

Know the Rules

Before you can begin to learn about coding in any language, WeDo included, you need to know that computer programming is about following rules. To some this may seem like work, but it's a lot like enjoying a fun game.

Rule 1: Coders must know what they want the computer to do and write a plan.

Rule 2: Coders must use special words to have the computer take **input**, make choices, and take action.

Rule 3: Coders need to think about what tasks can be put into a group.

Rule 4: Coders need to use **logic** with AND, OR, NOT, and other logic statements as key words.

Rule 5: Coders must explore the environment and understand how it works.

When you start a new WeDo project, you need to build the LEGO robot. It can be a project from the WeDo kit or one you think up yourself. Then you need to think about what you want the figure to do and how you might get it to do that task. You must do these steps before you're ready to code.

Know the Environment

Coders must understand the environment in which WeDo works. Shown here is the opening screen for the WeDo programming workspace. First notice the Save, Open, and Exit buttons that allow you to save new projects (your code for an activity) and return to them later. At the top left are a Recording button to let you record new sounds and items to let you know what is attached to your control module. Buttons here also let you get information.

Notice the red button at the bottom of the screen. It stops your program if you make one that just keeps running all the time. You can find out how the gears and other parts work by clicking on the buttons that look like LEGO blocks.

Breaking the Code

You can include sounds in your WeDo program. The sound is played on your computer, so you need speakers. You can test little parts of your code by moving the blocks into the coding window and using an arrow button or pressing the A key to start the program. Notice in the example shown here that the three sound blocks have different numbers, so you will hear sound 3 (honk!), then 1 (quack!), and then 3 again (honk!).

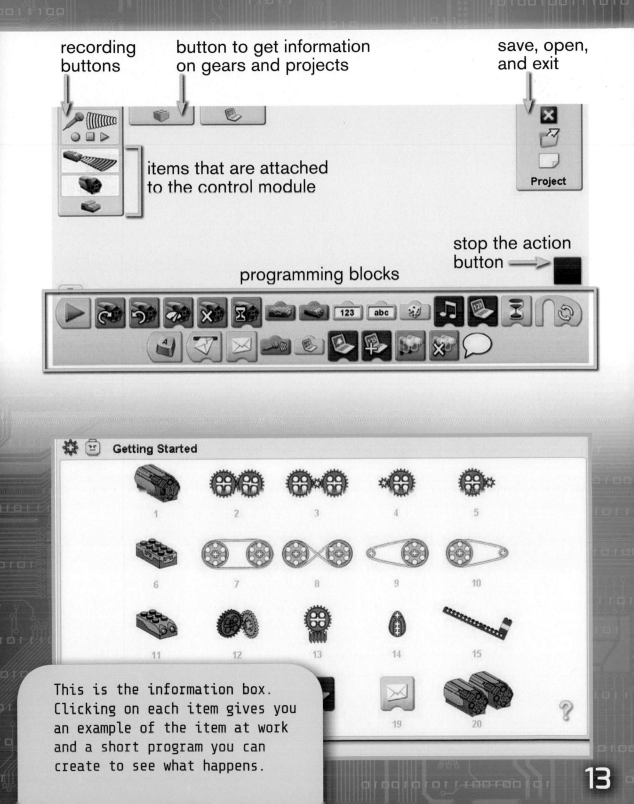

recording
buttons

button to get information
on gears and projects

save, open,
and exit

items that are attached
to the control module

Project

stop the action
button →

programming blocks

123   abc

Getting Started

1   2   3   4   5

6   7   8   9   10

11   12   13   14   15

19   20

This is the information box.
Clicking on each item gives you
an example of the item at work
and a short program you can
create to see what happens.

Time to Code

You can build a simple block and then add a motor with a propeller that turns. You need an axle to connect the motor to the blocks you will use for the propeller. Then you'll add the connection module and connect the motor's cord to it. But nothing happens until you write code to control the motor. Here's the code to turn the propeller slow in one direction and faster in the other direction.

Envelope blocks allow you to program two actions at once. A block with an envelope is used to start a line of code. The block with the mail slot starts the action. You can have more than one envelope/mail slot connection in your program. This programming shows two envelopes doing different things that will run at the same time. The notes play, and the motor turns.

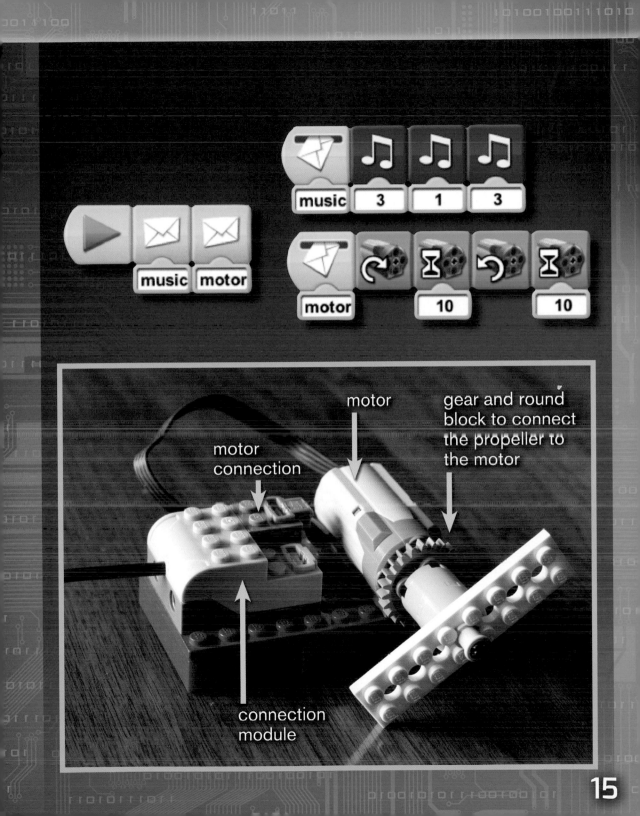

music   3   1   3

motor   10   10

music   motor

motor

gear and round
block to connect
the propeller to
the motor

motor
connection

connection
module

Chomp!

WeDo comes with directions for building several models. The directions for building the models are found right in the programming environment. You just have to click on the picture of the LEGO block and then on the picture of the LEGO minifigure head. Be sure to watch the introduction videos, which give some suggestions about what's going to happen.

One popular model is an alligator that closes its mouth when something moves in front of it. The mouth can move because it uses gears and **pulleys**, as well as a motion sensor in its mouth. The mouth must start open for the sensor to work. You can throw a LEGO into the mouth to make the sensor work!

This code makes the alligator go chomp when something passes in front of the sensor. It also makes a crunching sound. The code opens the mouth after a short time. Notice that the repeat block groups actions together, allowing them to loop, or repeat. This is a common practice for coders.

You Do with WeDo

WeDo kits give you many options, but you can use more LEGO parts than those in the kit to build and program your own project. The truck shown here was constructed using additional LEGO parts. The truck has a motion sensor on the front. We can program the truck to stop and back up when it's about to hit a LEGO wall.

The gearbox is upside down. Special pieces connect it to the truck.

The connection module is hidden here.

Notice the worm drive in the gearbox that touches a gear on the axle for the wheels.

Black connectors are used to connect the gearbox to the parts above it.

The motor is connected to the worm drive.

The USB connector plugs into the computer and sends power and information to the connection module. This allows the code you wrote to control the truck.

motion sensor to detect the wall

motor to turn the wheels so the truck can move

USB connector

Make It Move

We need to write code to make the truck move. Sometimes it's easier to write smaller pieces of code and then connect them into a single, longer line of code. This is helpful when testing the different parts before putting them together. After the small pieces of code do what you want them to, you can put the pieces together and see your whole program run.

Breaking the Code

Sometimes different programmers each do a small part of the code and then link their pieces together. They must all be sure they do their part according to the plan so the pieces fit together correctly and the finished code works properly.

The three pieces of code below each do something different. The first code makes the truck move forward until the sensor finds the wall, then it stops. The second code reverses the truck and stops it after 70 **revolutions**. Often you must try out different numbers in the timer boxes to get the results you want. The last code sends the truck forward again, but this time it travels 170 revolutions and then stops.

Sometimes plans change as you code. This longer line of WeDo code is a little different from the three shorter lines of code. It tells the truck to move forward until the sensor sees the wall. Then, it continues to move forward for another 70 revolutions and stops. The truck then backs up for 170 revolutions and stops.

Keep Coding!

Now you see how easy it is to code with WeDo. What do you think the following lines of code will make the truck do? Can you think of new lines of code for the truck?

Glossary

automate: To cause something to run on its own.

environment: The combination of computer hardware and software that allows a user to perform various tasks.

input: Information that is entered into a computer.

logic: A proper or reasonable way of thinking about or understanding something.

module: A part of a computer or computer program that does a particular job.

practical: Relating to real-world uses rather than what is imagined.

programming language: A computer language designed to give instructions to a computer.

pulley: A wheel with a groove on its edge that can fit a rope or belt, used to transfer power from a motor to other parts of a machine.

revolution: A turn around a central axis, as a wheel on an axle.

software: A program that runs on a computer and performs certain tasks.

USB port: An opening in a computer device that allows a wire to be plugged in to it, allowing the transfer of information and power between devices.

vehicle: An object that moves people from one place to another.

Index

Websites

Due to the changing nature of Internet links, PowerKids Press has developed an online list of websites related to the subject of this book. This site is updated regularly. Please use this link to access the list: www.powerkidslinks.com/kcc/wedo